Abundant Income, Abundant Life!

BECOMING A WORLD-CLASS FINANCIAL ADVISOR AT WORK AND HOME

Copyright © 2019 Curt Whipple

All rights reserved. No part of this publication may be reproduced or transmitted in any form by any means, electronic or mechanical, including photocopy, recording, or any other information storage and retrieval system, without permission in writing from the publisher.

First published by:

Financial Freedom Education Institute
Starting Point Publishing
41081 Ann Arbor Rd. E.
Plymouth, MI 48170
Phone: 734-844-3400

First Printing

ISBN: 9781691284467

Additional copies may be available at special discounts for bulk purchase in the U.S. for church groups, corporations, Institutions or other organizations. For more information, please contact: Financial Freedom Education Institute, 41081 Ann Arbor Rd. E. Plymouth, MI 48170. Phone: 734-844-3400

TABLE OF CONTENTS

Introduction v

Chapter one 1
What are Your Biggest Fears as a Financial Advisor or as an Insurance Representative?

Chapter Two 9
How Marketing is THE Key to Your Goals and Success

Chapter Three 19
Building Authority

Chapter Four 25
How You Can DOUBLE OR EVEN TRIPLE YOUR INCOME Starting Next Week!

Chapter Five 33
How to Spend Time in Meetings With Only Qualified Prospects and What To Tell the Others Who Don't Qualify?

Chapter Six 39
How to Get Around 100 New Referrals per Year?

Chapter Seven 47
The Secret Pond Few Are Fishing in that is Worth Millions

Chapter Eight 55
How You Can Run a 7 Figure Company and Only Work 25 Hours Per Week?

Chapter Nine..**65**
How to Create Systems and Processes That Run Your Practice and Give You More Free Time. Or, How I Don't Do Paperwork

Chapter Ten..**81**
How Your Office Environment (if you have an office) Can Help You Close Sales

Chapter Eleven **85**
Why Using the Help of a Coach/Mentor Can Be Key to Your Success.

Chapter Twelve **97**
Finding the Right Insurance Marketing Organization

Chapter Thirteen **105**
Looking Forward to Monday

Chapter Fourteen... **111**
Final Thoughts: How I Found Success In Life

Introduction

- Do you want more prospects to share with?
- Do you have a need for more income?
- Do you want to know how to build a 7 figure practice?
- Is your confidence fading away?
- Are you experiencing little-to-no growth on a yearly basis?
- Are you overwhelmed almost every day?
- Are you tired of doing and being responsible for everything?

- **Do you wish you could get more referrals?**

- **Do you feel that you are hitting the ceiling of your success and wish you knew the next step?**

- **Are you frustrated?**

THEN YOU'VE COME TO THE RIGHT PLACE! Here is just a sampling of what you will learn in this book:

- What most every advisor's greatest fears are and how to deal with each fear the right way. We will also look at how to overcome the fears you might be battling with and turn them into victories.

- We will talk about how you can build authority in your market! The younger you are, the harder it is to get potential clients to trust you as their financial advisor. They might be thinking you don't have enough experience to satisfy them. How can you overcome this? You'll find the answers here.

- Not only will we be talking about building authority at any age, but we will also be talking about how you can build that authority in as little as seven days. You did not misread that. In just 7 days!

- One of the most exciting things you will learn is how to double or even triple your income over last year, starting next week! We'll talk about how you can turn your current client files into the best year you have ever had financially.

- I will teach you how to get an average of 100 client referrals per year! How would that impact your income?

- Prospecting can sometimes be tedious. I will show you how you can actually get paid to prospect!

- I will share with you the things I did wrong over my 35 years in the financial services industry and how to avoid them. I will also be sharing all of the things I did right and how you can morph them into your own style.

- Together, I can help you design and achieve the lifestyle that you have always wanted. If you feel good about your current lifestyle, we will discuss how it can possibly be even better. If there is one thing I have learned, it is that most advisors work way too hard and make less money than if they learned how to make more money in less time.

- I will also be making a case for you to join a Masterclass group and how to find some terrific coaching so your life can be all you desire it to be, both at work and at home. Proverbs 27:17 states: "As iron sharpens iron so one man sharpens another." Let's begin a journey together and sharpen each other!

- Finally, I will be sharing how I became a financial success in our industry generating 2.7 million dollars of commissions and fees. I may not be the biggest advisory firm in America, but this book will help you work less, make more money and have more time with your family. It will help you find more time for matters of the heart and the spirit and be able to seek other things that God may be calling you to do with your life with the free time that you discover.

- My ultimate goal is that together we can serve others in more than just a financial way, but also in the way God designed us for, serving others in every way possible. I can't wait to get into all the details and hopefully, Lord willing, see your life change for the better and hear how you can impact lives in every way, even beyond financially.

CHAPTER ONE:
What are Your Biggest Fears as a Financial Advisor or as an Insurance Representative?

For many, it is the idea of being a failure or letting your family down, which is exactly what I was doing in the beginning.

I started my financial career like many of you reading this book. I sold life insurance for a small company out of Springfield, Illinois called Roosevelt National Life. After working with them for one year, they began asking me to take territories, hire new reps and train them.

In that new role, I created offices doing business in five states. I was traveling three weeks out of four on the road from Monday to Thursday and only seeing my family on Friday through the rest of the weekend. My daughter, Kelly, had just turned four and my wife, Connie, had just had our newborn son, Kristopher. The VP of the company came to me and said he wanted me to pick up what would be my sixth state. I quickly told him I couldn't do that and his reply was, *"if that's what we need you to do, that's what you will do."*

Two weeks later, after having just moved into our brand new home in Michigan, I put my resignation letter in the mail and quit. I had no other job lined up and our first house payment was due two weeks later. So, what did I do? As quickly as possible, I got my securities 7 license. Subsequently, I made a list of anyone we knew in the new area (which wasn't many) and began cold calling and asking them if they had ever thought of doing some financial planning.

I had AT&T install a phone line in my bare, cold and unfinished basement. Then with an old desk and a bare light bulb above my head, I started dialing for appointments. My very first month I made $5,000 and I said to myself, "I am so smart to have done this." That was until my second month, December of 1986, when I made only $250 per month.

Money became so tight that my blessed mother-in-law would come by and sneak a $20 bill in our mailbox. That was the best $20 I can ever remember. Every dollar counted.

I remember standing in the driveway of my home with my foot up on the bumper of my car and tears streaming down my face, sharing with my best friend Craig that I had no idea how I was going to make the next house payment. **I WAS LETTING MY FAMILY DOWN!** I don't believe anything can destroy a person more than letting their family down by not providing their needs.

Jumping ahead, I made it through those times with much prayer and time before God. From 1986 through 2001, I continued working out of the home, and at one point moved my office desk and file cabinets into our master bedroom! Talk about a great wife! Can you imagine her agreeing to that? We would wake up every morning and there, over by the bedroom window, sat all of my work. Okay, this is where you can call me a nut or dumkopf!

Obviously, that didn't last long. Finally, in 2001, I opened my own small office. In the late 1990's until the year 2001, I was making a decent living between $200,000 to $250,000 per year working out of the home. However, to do so, my family was once again paying the price of Dad working late nights *and doing it all:* marketing, prospecting, calling, appointment setting, multiple trips to prospects homes, filing, paperwork, paperwork and did I say paperwork? I worked as four employees all in one.

I felt like a real loser for many years and the enemy was constantly at the door of my mind telling me what a terrible husband and father I was in those early days. I will never forget juggling bills that would come in, doing the proverbial "robbing Peter to pay Paul" days.

That was when I discovered dinner events. Some of you reading this right now may want to turn me off as you can't stand the idea of dinner seminars. Maybe you have tried them and they just didn't work for you or you just don't like the idea of doing them. That's fine. Later, we will talk about other ways that you can build your business without seminars or dinners.

THE TURN-AROUND.

From 2001- 2008 my income grew from around $200,000 per year to over $2.7 million and I had

$1,000,000 in the company coffers.

What would your life and business look like if you made $2.7 million dollars a year? Want to find out? That's why I am writing this book.

MORE OBSTACLES.

Now the money is flowing and I have all the leads I could ask for. I focused on even bigger and better things. I kind of got full of myself thinking that I was something special because I was doing so well. I talked about opening three different offices in the Detroit Metro area. I was chasing every shiny object that would come my way that I thought would help me get bigger and better. So, what else could be the problem? A Lot!

In truth, I became overwhelmed and I had no time for my family. That meant I needed to hire some staff. No problem, I'll just drop an ad and hire one or two people. Only now, I am a manager, not just a financial advisor (some could call it a babysitter if you hire the wrong people). I was so busy chasing shiny objects thatI failed as a manager and seldom spent time investing in the lives of the people I hired. Office morale and motivation got low. I hired more people. Surely, that would have fixed the problem, but all I did was add to the mess already within the walls of the company.

Now I had a new set of problems. I was constantly trying to please every staff person. Because I was so busy and selling so much business, relationships with clients became a concern. I was in fear of compliance, industry regulations and potential legal issues that could arise. I started cheating family time wherever I could squeak in time to work. I seldom took much in the way of vacations. Even when I took a week, I was back working by the 4th day. I remember praying and asking God to help me, only He wasn't the one running my schedule... I was doing it all to myself!

HALLELUJAH!

I finally came to a point where I couldn't do it any longer. I informed my staff that I was going to be working only 25 hours per week and I placed the business in the hands of the Almighty. Whatever happened... happened. Then amazing things began. My staff took over. The two other advisors in my office stepped up. Amazingly, we continued to earn the same company income and now, I have a life and the freedom to spend time with my family. Each quarter now, I vacation for one week and every other weekend I take off Friday and spend time with my children and grandchildren. However, for this to happen there was a catch. Later I will tell you what the catch is and how you can make sure when this time comes for you, you don't blow it and almost lose your company as you build it.

I have been in the "Warrior" stage of my career for the past 35 years. It's been a time where I have been strong, energetic and ready to take on the world. As you've read, I have known what it's like to be broke and in debt and know what it is like to have plenty. Plenty is by far better. However, the greatest is having plenty of income AND plenty of free time to enjoy your family.

Now, I have a different goal as I enter what I hope to call the "Sage" stage of my life. My goal is to help others in the financial services and insurance industry, help them to achieve their own personal life goals, whatever that may be. It's not about making the most money. It's not about building the biggest company. It's about identifying what YOU want from your career and then helping you achieve YOUR dreams and goals. Helping you make enough money such that money is no longer an issue. Helping you find more time for your family. Helping you have a great career filled with happy clients, happy staff and lots of free time. Can I be the Sage in your career and life?

Now it's your turn. Let's move on to get you to your family, financial and business dreams!

CHAPTER TWO:
How Marketing is THE Key to Your Goals and Success

If there is one thing I have learned that makes all the difference in having an average income with an average lifestyle or having a 7 figure income and a fantastic lifestyle, it largely comes down to marketing.

Without "proper" marketing efforts, you will have no prospects to talk to. Of course, without prospects, you're in trouble.

Each person reading this book right now has special talents, yet you are all unique in where your talents lie.

FIRST THINGS FIRST: IDENTIFY YOUR STRENGTHS.

Are you:
- Outgoing and friendly?
- Easy to talk to?
- A great public speaker?
- An introvert?

If you are outgoing, friendly and easy to talk to, then your marketing may be best spent in the area of being out in the community, working with referrals, developing ways to promote yourself in mass media such as radio and TV.

If you are a great speaker, then public dinner events and speaking events, as well as mass media, should be your focus.

If you consider yourself to be an introvert, then you may market yourself best through referral programs and by providing the very best in service to your clients so they will brag about you. In most cases, you should consider social media and online marketing.

Regardless of your personality type, the number one key to marketing yourself or your company is to build with **"Authority Marketing."**

Prospects want to know what makes you different from all of the other financial professionals out there. Why should they do business with you? Why is your idea the right path to financial freedom?

If you are seen as an authority in the securities and/or insurance field, then prospects are more open to hearing what you have to share regardless of where your strengths mentioned above lie. So again, here's the question... *what makes you different?*

The best way to share with others how you differ from everyone else is through a USP. I have heard USP mean several different things. But to me, it best stands for your "Unique Selling Points".

Here's my USP:

> "I help financial planners and life insurance agents get more 'qualified' prospects, double and even triple the size of new business per client, gain up to 100 referrals per year and make their life simpler for more time with family and loved ones."

My goal going forward is to be someone who would help you become all you were meant to be.

THE 3 M'S

You must be able to state in a simple phrase what makes you different or unique. Not everyone will respond to it. However, I know you will get more response by separating yourself from others in securities and insurance and that comes from three key areas. Your **Market**, your **Message**, and your **Media**.

AREA #1 – YOUR MARKET

You must find people who are "starving" for what you wish to share with them and teach them. DO NOT DETERMINE YOUR MESSAGE UNTIL YOUR MARKET IS CRYSTAL CLEAR AND AS SPECIFIC AS POSSIBLE. Too many advisors are trying to reach everyone who can fog a mirror and have money to invest. As a result, most reps skip right to the media they want to use and end up with an approach that is far too broad to finding the ideal prospect. I've heard, "Oh, I heard radio is the way to go." Another thinks direct mail is the only way. The conversation goes something like this: "I need more prospects… so, maybe I should take out a newspaper ad… maybe I should throw up a website… maybe I should send out a direct mail sales letter."

The way to properly choose your target market is to start with GEOGRAPHIC. However, targeting solely on a geographic area is like getting in a plane and dropping flyers and hoping one hits the right person.

The second step after geographic is to think of DEMOGRAPHICS. For most advisors they immediately state they want to reach people near or in retirement, ages 55 to 70. Why? Because they believe they are the ones with the most money. While this may be your desired market, keep your mind open to other options. I will talk about this more in a bit. In addition, you should be thinking about incomes that your ideal market is earning. How about family size, home value, married or single, divorced, female, male or both? Get as specific as you can when identifying your ideal market.

Finally, you must identify your target markets PSYCHOGRAPHICS. Demographics and Psychographics will allow you to identify your ideal prospect. Here are some tips from Dan Kennedy's book *Magnetic Marketing*:

- What keeps them awake at night, staring at the ceiling, unable to fall asleep as it relates to what you have to offer them?

- What are they most frustrated about at their current age as it relates to your business?

- What is causing them pain right now, as it relates to financial services that you provide?

- What is the single biggest problem you can solve for them?

- What do they secretly, privately desire most as it relates to money and their goals?

To identify the answer to this last bullet, get 6-8 of your best clients and invite them to a lunch or dinner on you. Let them know you need their advice and you will be looking to them as an advisory board to help you answer some key questions they may be feeling now or have felt in the past. Have some questions prepared to ask and let them help you identify the answers to what they secretly, privately desire most about their retirement. I think you will be shocked at how many of the answers have nothing to do with money.

Another path is to go on LinkedIn and join some forums for the target market you are seeking to reach (ie: seniors).

Once you do this you are ready to move onto the "Message."

AREA #2 – YOUR MESSAGE

> **KEY:** Your Message Must Be Crystal Clear And Finely-Crafted Before You Even BEGIN to Consider The Media You Will Use To Communicate It.

Answer the following:

- What is unique about my product?
- What is unique about my presentation?
- What is unique about my service?
- What industry norms do I "legally" bend or break?
- What is unique about my personality?
- What is my story?
- Who or what are my enemies?
- What is unique about my best clients?

If you can't come up with some clear answers to those questions, you're going to need to make some changes to your business. Period. This is critical. Do not move on without doing this and identifying these key questions!

Now that you have identified what makes you different from every other advisor and agent, you want to write out a message that will attract people who most likely will respond to that uniqueness and also disqualify the ones who don't.

- Who qualifies?
- What makes them qualify?
- What age group are they in?
- How much money do they make?
- Where do they live?

For many reps, they all fish in the same pond i.e: Age 50-70, $100,000 of income having lots of bank CDs! If you have your uniqueness well displayed, you don't have to be afraid of this large pond. Later I will teach you how to find a pond that few if any others are fishing in. Whooo-Hooo! There's a lot of fish in there and only your hook will likely be the one in the pond.

A fun way to identify your message is to write it as if you were writing a personal ad. *Here's one that is tongue in cheek, but you'll get the idea.*

> Awesome and unique advisor seeks rich married or single people who want to retire without fear or concern over money. I will help you travel the world, walk the

beaches of your dreams, spend gobs of money on your grandchildren and make your wife happily married to you. I am able to do this by uniqueness #1, uniqueness #2, #3 etc.

Your message needs to have a Call to Action (CTA) to be effective. A call to action comes by offering something that your ideal prospect would want.

Free reports, demos, videos of information, teleseminars, free guides, webinars, checklists, calculators, anything that helps your prospect raise their hand and say "I'd like that" and or "solve a problem they have".

What can you offer, give away, or deliver, such that when accepted, will allow you to separate the wheat from the chaff?

AREA #3 – YOUR MEDIA

Now ask, where do my ideal prospects hang out? Are they watching certain TV programs? Are they listening to specific radio shows? What restaurants do they love? What kind of magazines do they love to read? Is there a certain type of mail they like to receive and read?

The key to effective marketing is to make sure your marketing dollars are going to the areas with the highest concentration of your ideal prospect and the best chance of a high return on your dollar invested. Shot-gun marketing is the key to failure and frustration.

CHAPTER THREE:
Building Authority

One way to separate yourself from every other representative in the marketplace is by building your authority and being the person that your prospects look at and say "I want him/her to help me with my wealth."

ARTICLES

One way to do so is to write articles for submission to magazines and newspapers that your prospects read or respect. These publications are always looking for content each day, week or month.

But Curt, I'm not much of a writer. You don't need to be. There are people in the marketplace called Ghost-Writers. This means they will scour the internet looking for good material on your behalf and write an article for you for a fee. You would review the article, make your own custom changes to it and then submit it.

There is a mail list you can get on called Haro (www.helpareporter.com) where reporters and writers put out requests for articles on certain subjects. By getting on such a list, you can reply to someone seeking help in writing an article and submit your article as a possibility to fill their need. You will almost always get a copy of the article when published. When you get a copy, you can put the content on your website and equally mail out to your clients. You can even frame it in your office. *If securities licensed, make sure it gets compliance approved before submitting to the journalist.*

AUTHOR

Probably one of the most impressive ways to build authority is to author a book. This is my third book and while I typed every word of all my three books, you don't have to do it that way.

The first key to writing a book is to know that the objective is not to sell your book. The odds of writing a book that a major book publisher would want is slim to none and most likely you would not sell enough (besides to your mother and your closest friends) to make it worth your time.

The reason to write a book is that it acts as a brochure but does much more. Anyone can hand out a business card or a brochure or flyer. That doesn't create any authority. Now, a book is a different animal altogether. A book makes you an "instant" authority figure in your area of expertise

The book becomes something you give away to every person you meet. Always carry a couple in your briefcase for someone you meet on a plane or in a restaurant. When you learn how to build your referral marketing program (coming later), always send out a free book with your note. You can give two books to your new clients. Clients love to hand their friends your book and be able to say "This is a book written by my personal advisor and I thought you might enjoy it so I picked up a copy for you".

Another way to build authority (and one you should put as number one on your priority list) is to go to *www.postupstands.com* and get a 6-foot poster of yourself professionally done. You might say "Curt, that isn't me. Isn't that a bit narcissistic"? It's not at all. It's one more step in creating an image and authority. Do other reps have that in their office? No? Isn't the idea to separate yourself from the rest of the pack? Now, if you have a foyer or if you are off a hallway, put it in the foyer or hallway. This banner is also powerful if you are doing dinner events and educational events. Make sure the post-up stand is at the entry to the meeting.

Whenever I speak or do a dinner event, everyone gets a copy of my book. Whenever they come in for their appointment, it amazes me how many of them have fully read my book and even highlighted and made notes in it. They come in already sold and simply want to go through the process. When I do TV interviews, the air personalities and even the camera people all get a copy of my book as well as the station manager.

The second key when you write your book is that it must have a call to action (CTA) throughout and at the end.

By the way, for anyone who is reading this book, here is a call to action:

WOULD YOU LIKE TO KNOW HOW TO WRITE YOUR FIRST BOOK IN JUST 7 DAYS? IF SO, THEN JUST SEND ME AN EMAIL AT

curt@myadvisorsuccess.com

AND REQUEST IT AND I WILL RUSH OUT YOUR FREE BOOK WITH ALL THE DETAILS ON HOW TO DO SO.

By the way, I'm serious! Send me an email and I will be happy to rush out your copy of a book written by my friend Darcy Juarez. It will teach you how to write your first book *in just 7 days*. I used the lessons while writing this book. It's your gift from me. It's absolutely free just by emailing me at

curt@myadvisorsuccess.com.

This is not a download, it is an actual book I will mail at my cost **FREE** but you must ask for it.

CHAPTER FOUR:
How You Can DOUBLE OR EVEN TRIPLE YOUR INCOME Starting Next Week!

I have used many of the standard financial software programs available to financial professionals. The problem by using these software programs was it guaranteed me to be in the big pond with every other advisor and agent. I was a commodity who looked and presented like every other advisor in my area.

There are four main software programs used by financial professionals. Take a minute. I bet you could easily name the top two if not the top four.

Question: Why would you want the most popular software programs that make your presentation just like everyone else?

What do most software programs print out for your prospect? 30, 40 maybe even 50 pages or more? What I learned by using these programs are three things:

- First, they didn't make me unique.

- Second, they left the client in a state of confusion as there was just too much to remember and consume.

- Thirdly, they were 95% fluff and template stuff and only 5% content.

After going through a lot of money and time to learn each program, I decided to create mine. Now, this is where it gets hard for me. I did not write this book in an effort to sell my software program. As a matter of fact, I give 100% of the proceeds from this program to charity. I just wanted something that would help me close more sales and help other advisors do the same. Be aware that our industry is much like any other industry. I believe most advisors are sincere about truly helping those they come in contact with (PS: those are the only ones I want to help). Unfortunately, there are many in our industry today for only one reason and that is the almighty dollar. They will say anything to get a prospect to become a client. It really doesn't matter if it is the BEST thing or not. For those that ruin our industry name, they get high off the thrill of the sale rather than a high off the thrill of serving others. If you represent the ones that are in it solely for the money, then please throw this book away.

Please don't share an interest in the software I am about to talk about.

The name of the software is Red, Blue, Green concepts. You can go to *www.RBGconcepts.com* and learn more about it if you would like.

One of the keys to RBG is that it is only a six-page report! Yet everything you need to help a client make good decisions will be in those 6 pages. I created the software in 2002 and immediately saw the impact of using it. Immediately I had clients telling me how much they wanted to invest with me and gave me guidelines on where they wanted it invested and how much in each area. Since it was their ideas and decisions and not mine (by trying to sell them on my ideas), they invested more of their assets with my firm, if not all of their assets.

I happen to be a big fan of indexed annuities in place of bonds at this time. I think that rising interest rates will hurt the bond market. As of this writing, I am excited about the future of the market as well. By using this software, clients tell me what percent of their money they want in green, blue and red investments. My firm went from bringing in 8-10 million clients assets per year to 20-30 million per year. We could probably do even more, but the lifestyle is important to everyone at our firm. Now we can work with fewer clients and still produce high volumes of investment sales. Recently we had one client invest $1.2 million into index annuities, and $1.6 million in AUM and when the wife retires at the end of this year they will have another $2.5 million to invest with us. This all came from RBG and a 6-page report.

Our AUM (assets under management) have continued to soar as well as commissions and we did it with fewer clients and by "helping" our client's do what was the right thing for them. Don't get me wrong. If a client told me what they wanted to do and I felt they were making a mistake by overweighing one area over another, I quickly encouraged them along a more reasonable path.

Here's what a few advisors have shared with me about RBG:

"After struggling for years to win clients using various planning tools, some simple and some complex, I have found the Red, Blue, Green platform to be nearly miraculous in its effectiveness. The PDF output, when properly presented, catches the prospects' attention and – more importantly – doesn't confuse them. They understand not only what you are showing them, but how novel and valuable you are compared with other advisors they work with. As an added bonus, the time it takes to set up a client in the software is far less than the other platforms I've used."

— *Drew K., Washington*

"Red, Blue, Green is the single most important tool that I have ever had in my practice of over 15 years… hands down bar none. This one program has done more to help me close business than anything I have ever used. I would strongly recommend Red Blue Green to anyone and everyone in the financial industry."

— *K. R., Tennessee*

"Even though RBG's platform is simple, the final product is anything but; my clients walk away from my office with a finished product that is professional and well organized – the graphics and documentation create a well-rounded presentation that concretely outlines my client's current financial situation and suggested financial situation. I highly recommend RBG Concepts, from start to finish."

— *M. F., Michigan*

"Using Red, Blue, Green has made complex issues simple for prospects to understand. The prospect will tell me what they want instead of me trying to convince them about what they should have. At the end of the day, it's really all about how someone feels emotionally about their financial situation - and RBG is the simplest, yet complete explanation I have ever come across. Use it and the sales will follow...."

— *M. S., New Mexico*

HOW YOUR EXISTING CLIENT'S FILES CAN AND WILL MAKE THIS FINANCIALLY YOUR BEST YEAR EVER WITHOUT SPENDING ONE DIME ON MARKETING.

Prior to utilizing RBG software, I would get clients who would give me $100,000 for an annuity and maybe $100,000 for AUM. Well, that was nice. However, that meant I needed more leads to sell more too. It resulted in me running my tail off with a high number of clients and little in the way of investments. I think you'll agree with me that sometimes the larger clients are easier to work with than the smaller ones. I was overwhelmed with small clients.

OVERWHELMED IS ANOTHER WORD FOR POOR SERVICE!

If you are going to spend the right amount of time servicing your clients, you need two things.

1. Fewer clients
2. Clients investing more assets with you… per client. I have found that using RBG has helped me accomplish these two areas.

FOR EVEN FASTER GROWTH NEXT WEEK…

Hold a client event for your existing clients (especially your "A" clients) and share your new software program with them ensuring they see the value of it. Advise each person to set up a time to come back in for a review and build a brand new plan for them using RBG. You will be amazed how many clients will decide to move more money to you to help them with!

By the way, what did this cost you? It cost you a room rental with some cookies and coffee. Or, if you skip the big meeting, just start doing an RBG on each client you review with going forward in your office.

Let's assume you review with your existing clients and 35 invest an average of $100,000 with you in annuities. That would be $3.5 million in **EXTRA** annuity sales for the year. If they invested all of that in AUM, wouldn't that be exciting? You bet!

Be prepared for some exciting sales growth. Oh, lest I forget, did I tell you it is one of the easiest software programs you could ever learn? I mean how hard can it be with six pages? Once you check out the website, feel free to call me if you would like to discuss it in more detail.

CHAPTER FIVE:
How to Spend Time in Meetings With Only Qualified Prospects and What To Tell the Others Who Don't Qualify?

I mentioned earlier that I predominantly do dinner seminars to attract new clients in addition to referrals. I do this because I feel that one of the main gifts I am blessed with is the gift of teaching. I love to speak and share with groups even more than a one on one teaching (and I love that part also).

Whatever seminar or system that you use to present to groups, it is the close and the CTA (call to action) that can make all the difference. Remember, people care about one thing "WIIFM" (what's in it for me). If your close doesn't address that, then you will get a poor response.

While I won't be discussing closing in this book, I did want to tell you one thing I do that saves me a ton of hours. Equally, it gives me the confidence that I can help someone before spending an hour in my office only to discover they have no intention of working with me or need my help other than the free advice they can grab while wasting my time and theirs.

I have always mentioned in my workshops and interviews that I will work with anyone regardless of their financial position. The reason I say this is based on my Christian beliefs. I believe one day I will stand before God when my time on this earth is complete. I would not know how to answer God when He looks back over my life and asks me, "Why didn't you help John Doe?" How do I look at the face of God and say, "He didn't have enough money!" That goes against everything I believe. While I choose to help anyone seeking my help, it doesn't have to equate to charity each time.

So, when I close I tell everyone that **I WILL NOT BE OFFERING THEM A FREE CONSULTATION** (talk about unique)! I tell the audience you have only one decision to make tonight and that is "have you heard enough that you feel it would be worth a 15-20 minute phone call with me?" I say, "May I be straight? I don't want to waste your precious time and I also don't want to waste my time. So tonight if you tick the box 'yes', you will be saying, 'let's talk by phone, Curt.' On the call, you will be able to ask me questions and I will ask you questions that we would not discuss in this room with others here. If I believe I can help you and you feel good about the confidential call we have, then we can arrange a time for you to stop in my office for a visit."

Thereafter, they fill out our response form and turn it in. I do set the phone calls up at the seminar as I walk out with the appointments I desire by phone.

WHAT I DO WHEN THEY DON'T QUALIFY

About 10-20% of the people who set up a call may not qualify to meet with me. What do I mean by qualify? They have no assets or certainly very little in the way of assets and little ways to save more. Here is my reply to them on the call: "John and Mary, I would love to help you and I know I can do quite a bit to make sure you are on the right track. It would take me some time to do a full analysis for you and I charge $500 for the meeting or meetings if it took more than one." To date, in all the years in business, I had one person take me up on the fee.

Please note, I truly do want to help those who are broke or have little in the way of investments. However, if they can't even come up with $500 to lay out a plan to build wealth, then I believe they aren't that serious. But it wouldn't surprise me if they have cable TV, a big screen and the latest model car!

KEYS TO THE SALE WHEN THEY COME IN

Present more benefits and less time on features.

Let's say you need to purchase a new suit. You walk into the first clothing store and as you stand in front of the mirror, the salesperson begins to tell you all the features of this new suit. It has double stitching in the seams. It is made out of 100% wool and has a guarantee of holding its color for 3 years without fading.

You go to a second store and try on the suit. The salesperson quickly pinches a little of the suit together at your waistline, making your physique look more like the hulk (or at least you think so).

He straightens out the shoulders and then tells you how powerful and successful you look in that suit.

Which suit are you more likely to buy? The one emphasizing the benefits of how it makes you look and feel!

Remember, everyone cares about one thing... WIIFM. I want to know what your service will do to improve my life!

Let's take that to a securities rep selling mutual funds. Rep number one pulls out the Morningstar report and shows you how the fund he/she recommends compared to the SP 500 over the last 20 years. Rep number two may do the same but then follows up with saying that this fund has been the most consistent fund in its class which means that you can depend on it for years and years of steady income. Or, with this steady income, you should have no problem funding your children's education. Or the rep states that while not guaranteed, it has an excellent chance of meeting your dream income for your retirement years. Do they want the best Morningstar rating or the one that best provides the benefits that they desire? Who gets the sale?

CHAPTER SIX:
How to Get Around 100 New Referrals per Year?

I have found two good ways to get referrals from my clients. Of course, it starts with doing a great job for them and truly listening to them and understanding their needs and goals and showing them a way to achieve them. I also believe that doing dinner seminars and or client events is important within the referral system and I will explain why.

METHOD ONE:

ASK! Wow, that was worth the price of this book! I built my early career by asking for them. Here is how it would go;

Me: "Well Bob and Jane, congratulations on a very good decision and I want to welcome you to the C. Curtis Financial Family! I am so excited for you giving me the opportunity to serve you and I want you to know that the service doesn't stop here. Over the next 12 months, I or any of the staff of C. Curtis Financial may be calling you to set up four quarterly visits to review your progress and give you the confidence in the decision you are making today. We like to meet four times. The first year as I am new to you and you are new to us. We want to build a relationship that will last for years to come while helping you secure your income and retirement.

In the second year and on, now that we have gotten to know each other better, we convert to semi-annual reviews, as we find it is more reasonable to judge performance going forward every six months instead of three months.

Bob, Jane, my passion in life is helping people reach (or have) a retirement that provides all of the income they will need, do it tax efficiently and be financially secure to travel and spend lots of time with their family. If I don't find the people to talk to, then my dream of helping others crashes and many will lose the joy of having all that they've hoped and dreamt for because we never met.

I depend on my family of clients to share what they have found as a result of our meeting with others that I might never have the opportunity to meet and help.

(While I am saying this, I slowly pull out my referral book and set it on the table. I place their name on the top of a fresh page and then while talking write down in the left side 1, 2, 3.)

So, Bob and Jane, I would like to invite you to one of my future dinner events as my guest, as well as three other people that you may know that would likely enjoy learning what you have learned. I will send them a special invitation to attend, and with your permission, mention your name as part of our family of clients. In the same way, you never felt pressure I am sure they won't either. This way you have helped your friends and then they can make their own decision."

(Now as I ask the next question, I look down and place the pen just to the right of the number one. While asking the question, I do not look at them at this time)

"Bob and Jane, what's the first name that comes to your mind?"

> There are three important things here that must be understood.
> 1. Under any circumstances, you do not write down more than three numbers at this time
> 2. Do *not use* a yellow notepad. Instead, use a small journal.
> 3. Never ask for a phone number or address yet

By using a small journal, it is not as scary to them as a notepad which then makes them think "Oh-my-gosh" is he going to make us fill up this entire notepad? You only want three names to start with, and then they see that it might not be hard to think of three.

As soon as they give me two names, I then write down #4 and #5. When they give me 3 and 4, I then write down 6 and 7. I do this until they stop and say they can't think of anyone else. I have had people take out their cell phones and start flipping through names and hear the wife say, "Oh Bob, how about Jim and Beth? My record was one couple who gave me 27 names!

HOW TO INVITE THE NEW NAMES

You do a **THREE STEP LETTER CAMPAIGN** (not email!!!)

Emails are quickly scanned and they could be deleted and never read as they don't know who you are. When people receive an addressed letter by hand (**KEY**), they tend to always open it. Now it is a question of how well written your letter is.

I highly recommend that if you have never heard of the "NO B.S. Inner Circle" before, that you contact me to check it out

curt@myadvisorsuccess.com

As a member of Dan's team, I will help you grow your marketing knowledge and become a marketing superstar and you can learn about a 3 step letter campaign and how to write and implement one

METHOD TWO:

The Partners Program

In 2008, I wanted to find another way for prospects to introduce people to myself and our firm. That's when I created what we call the **Partners'**

Program. On each desk in our offices, there is a plastic stand with an 8 ½ x 11 flyer in it introducing our Partners' Program to everyone.

If a couple were to say to me "Curt, although we are thrilled with what you have done for us, we just aren't comfortable handing out any other names to you at this time," I tell them I respect their decision.

I then point to the flyer standing on my desk and say by the way, by being a new client this quarter, you qualify to join us on our next Partners' Program event. At the time of this writing, our next event is a cruise on a yacht where we will have a wonderful dinner and live music while cruising the Detroit River and seeing sights of Downtown and the Canadian side of the river. It truly is a magical event.

We've taken 50 clients on a bus to see the Beach Boys in Concert. We've been to see Cirque Du Sole' on ice. We've been to the Fisher Theater to see the Broadway play "Grease" just to name a few.

These events have been such a success that many clients who, prior to the event never knew each other, became friends at the event. Before leaving the event, we hand them a flyer of what our next event is.

When I handed the flyer for Cirque du Sole' to one couple, the wife elbowed her husband in the ribs and said, "Who do we know that we can refer to Curt? Because I am not missing Cirque du Sole!"

You see, by becoming a client they are invited to the next event automatically. We never mention the event during the selling process. Instead, we wait until they decide to become a client. Once they come to an event, they see how great these events are and often times, they want to attend the next one. To attend another event, we kindly ask them to consider sending us a referral to either a dinner event or an educational event. Either way, they qualify.

Our first Partners' event, we had 8 people. The next one we had around 12 people until finally, we averaged between 30 and 50 people each quarter. This means that we received that quarter somewhere between 20 and as high as 40 referrals each quarter. Now multiply that by 4 quarters.

Between these two methods, you should never have to worry again about enough people to talk to.

If you would like to learn more about this referral program go to my website

www.MyAdvisorSuccess.com

Click on Secrets to 100 Client Referrals Per Year.

CHAPTER SEVEN:
The Secret Pond Few Are Fishing in that is Worth Millions

If you have ever conducted a dinner event, you will know that virtually every financial advisor is after the same crowd, especially those between the age 50-70 years. Why? They believe that these folks have all the money. What if you were told there was another pond that I have been fishing in (and you can too), that virtually no planners or agents are going after? What if I told you I could get more people to attend this event who seldom if ever get an invite by any financial professional and I can send fewer mailers and get just as big of a crowd?

I'm talking about the 40-55 year old age group (most of which tend to be in their 40's). Here's the shocker. In most cases, they have more money to invest than the older clients I served the majority of my career.

I had one couple come in with $5.35 million of which they could only invest just under $3 million as the rest was tied up in the wife's 401K plan at the time (which by the way as I am proof reading this, she retired and just rolled over the rest of their $2.35 million). They invested everything they could with us. Another couple came in with $3.2 million and invested 100% of it with us. I can't begin to tell you the number of cases that have all been million-dollar cases which came from this age group that few seem to be serving.

Why do I think these prospects end up investing all of their assets with us? For one, the RBG software makes it easy for them to make decisions. Secondly, they haven't been to 10 dinner events in the past and had spoken with over 7 advisors and gotten totally confused by all of the different opinions and recommendations. Why? Because of their age no one else is sending them invitations!

Now get ready… what did the mailer I sent out to this age group talk about? Investments? Nope. Annuities? Nada. Social Security? No way. RMD's? They could care less at their age. I talked about Indexed Universal Life Insurance or what I call LIRP's (Life Insurance Retirement Plans)

The entire event was centered around good ole' fashioned life insurance.

HOW WOULD YOU LIKE TO GET PAID TO PROSPECT?

That's what this dinner event does. You see, most of these folks are maxing out their 401k's and 403b's because their tax advisor told them it was the way to go. My problem with that is that as I write this, we are in one of the lowest tax brackets in American history for anyone earning or making less than $300,000 dollars per year. Why would anyone want a deduction off their income if they are in the 15, 22 or 24% tax bracket now?

At the time of this writing, our country has debt of about $21 trillion. To put that in perspective, if you took just $1 trillion "seconds" on your wristwatch it equals 32,000 years!! Now multiply that by 21. Gheez! Do you really think that somewhere down the road taxes won't be going back up?

You say "Yeah but Curt, people will most likely be in a lower tax bracket when they retire." Really? Do most of the prospects you work with want to live on less money in retirement than they do now? Is someone making $160,000 per year now going to say they want to retire on $75,000? That would be a rare case indeed. They may say they could retire on $110,000 instead of 160, but guess what? Whether 160K or 110K they are still in the 22% tax bracket. That's not a smaller bracket and that's if tax rates never go up. The way our government likes to spend money, I don't see them cutting back taxes any time soon. Rather, I believe taxes will be going up.

Let's say a 30-year-old decides to put away $500 per month ($6,000/yr) in their 401K and for simplicity sake, they are in a 24% tax bracket. That means the amount they will save on their taxes the first year will be $1,440 ($6,000 X .24). If they did that for 30 years, their total tax savings by age 60 comes to $43,200. Not bad.

However, let's say their 401K is now rolling to an IRA and is worth about $600,000 and they want to take a 5% interest income from it to supplement their retirement. That would be an additional income from their pre-tax retirement savings during retirement of $30,000. The problem is they have never paid taxes on this income, and if they still (don't hold your breath) were only in the 24% bracket 30 years later at age 60, that would be a tax of $7,200 per year and they would have a net income of only $22,800. If they lived until 90 years of age (for 30 years after retirement) and paid $7,200 per year, **they would end up paying $216,000 back to the IRS.**

Let me get this straight... the IRS allows them to keep $43,200 during their working years and in return the IRS gets back $219,000. Who won? Not the investor!

I teach people in this seminar and in the lower brackets (in some cases even the higher brackets) to invest only up to what the company matches and then put the rest into a LIRP. It only makes sense.

> You might ask why not recommend a Roth instead? Two reasons;
>
> 1. They are limited in what they can contribute to a Roth and many of the prospects from these seminars are maxing out their 401K to the tune of $18,500 to $24,500 per year. They may only get a

match of maybe 3-5% or say $5,000. So, they might be putting in $19,500 without a match. They are building, as famous author and CPA Ed Slott likes to say, **a tax time bomb.**

2. Most people will invest their Roth at risk in the stock market, whereas the LIRP has no downside risk. Today, there are LIRP's with no upside caps on earnings and no downside risk. How can a Roth at risk compete with that?

Remember the income from a LIRP when taken as a loan is tax-free. The LIRP will blow away the 401K in income potential every time.

Ok, so the prospect comes in to talk with you about the LIRP. For me to do a proper job and make sure it is right for them, I have to know about their other assets. I TREAT THIS FIRST APPOINTMENT LIKE ANY OTHER APPOINTMENT THAT WASN'T COMING IN OFF AN LIRP SEMINAR. Same Q&A time, same RBG presentation but of course the addition of an IUL quote.

I had a doctor who came in from my LIRP seminar with their spouse and the first thing they did was put $827,000 into a Fixed Indexed Annuity. They came back this past week and transferred another $1,227,000 into AUM. They also agreed to start the LIRP.

So, if someone says they will take 8% of their $150,000 salary and move it from 401K to IUL, and the $12,000 premium results in a $6,000 commission and I still in addition to that get almost two million of assets, I call the LIRP program as "getting paid to prospect."

How can someone who has an insurance only license build a saleable practice? It is by selling LIRP's and setting up residual income. What's another way an insurance licensed person can build even more residual income?

Set a goal of how much income you need to make in a year. Let's say it is $250,000. If you sold $3.5 million of annuities, you would be there (remember that by using what I am teaching you, you should have much larger sales than you have experienced before). If you get even more prospects with my systems, then it is a no-brainer to do $3.5 million.

Now, assume by using what I am teaching to you and presenting it in a way that makes the complex simple and the prospects decisions easier, you were able to reach that 3.5 million mark by September that year. So, why not set up all future annuity sales for the balance of that year as commission level "C" sales? Now you could earn a couple of percent up front and a trail commission for the next 9-14 years until the end of the surrender period! Then, in the second year with the trails now coming in from the last 12 months, you only need $3.2 million before you go to a trail. This means, each year you would have a larger and larger trail commission, until finally after ten to fourteen years, you would have a steady income each and every year. **NOW YOU HAVE AN INSURANCE PRACTICE TO SELL!** If you are young enough, sell your practice and invest your big payday and then move somewhere else and do it again. Any idea what your ultimate nest egg would look like if you built a few insurance practices and sold each of them during your working years?

CHAPTER EIGHT:
How You Can Run a 7 Figure Company and Only Work 25 Hours Per Week?

I f I told you that you could earn $400,000 to $500,000 or more per year and work only 25 hours per week, who would raise their hand and say "I'm in"!?

If you didn't call me for the name of a psychologist! Having income and a lot of free time for family and friends is an amazing lifestyle. It's really simple, *but I wouldn't say it is easy.*

There could only be three reasons why an owner would not make that happen:

1. You love what you do so much and it's a contest for you to see how big you can grow it. While that's a fine goal, you

probably (in my opinion) won't live long enough to truly enjoy what you've built due to too much stress along the way.

2. You don't know how to do it.

3. You won't delegate in your business and are not willing to trust other people or staff (which means you should fire them immediately and find someone you can trust). If you don't you will never be free!

By the way, I think number three is what any entrepreneur struggles with, including me. We start by ourselves, many times out of our home and we bust our butts to build this thing and it is exceedingly hard to let some parts of it go, in order to grow. However, when we do this, WE are the cog or governor of the growth of the company because it can't go any further as everything (or most everything) depends on us.

I remember a time when I was at my Broker/Dealer conference. A younger rep was sitting in front of me. At break time, he turned around and asked me about my business. I mentioned to him the staff I have and his reply was, "As soon as I make a little bit more money, then I am going to hire someone to help me." I replied back, "You've got it backward. As soon as you hire someone to help you, then you will begin to make more money and grow."

I remember when I just had three staff people including myself as the only advisor. Only one staff member was full-time staff and the other two were part-timers. My wife came to me and said she met a young Morgan Stanley rep in the mall while shopping with my daughter. My daughter knew the guy from a Bible study she attended and my wife said I should talk to him about coming to work for me. I remember that my reply was **"How am I going to do that? I'm so busy right now I don't have the time to train him."** Does that sound familiar?

To make a long story short, I did hire him and while it took a while for us to grow (as he was sitting in meetings with me and learning), he shortly began starting to do his own meetings and then, my business took off. As stated before, now I have two other reps in my firm. I certainly couldn't do $2.7 million of revenue and bring in $25-$30 millions of new assets in a year by myself and would be surprised if you said you are.

THINKING LONG TERM

Another reason to hire other reps in your firm is to plan for your retirement. I have had several offers to sell my firm. I turned them down for a number of reasons. Chief amongst those reasons is that I truly care about my clients. If I sold to most securities reps, their goal would be to come in and depending on the business, they will convert all of my client's conservative assets to AUM and market risk. Since I am a fan of Index Annuities, as one part of my client's future, it's hard to turn them over to someone else with a different idea that I believe could hurt them in the long run, especially if they are already retired.

A BIG MISTAKE

In 2012, I was 57 years old and I was just starting to think about someday in the future selling my firm. At the time I had two other young advisers who had been working with me for some time (not the current advisors I now have on the team). While they were both great salespeople and I liked and even cared for them like sons. I felt that one of them was just not the right fit to own the company someday, even though he had been with the company for ten years. I had received some complaints from staff and a few clients. I knew that he was hoping to move to North Carolina so I took him out for a cup of coffee before Christmas in 2012. I told him I didn't feel that he was the right person to take over the company but I told him I would give him $50,000 to help him move to North Carolina and get a start. I also said I would fly down and do whatever I could to help him and make sure he succeeded.

Unfortunately, he decided to make a different move. Almost 5 months later, in April of 2013, I came into the office and found his office space cleaned out. The following Tuesday, a client came in with a postcard from this rep saying "Come to the Grand Opening of my New Office (which was about 1 mile down the road from my office).

My mistake was not that I met him for coffee and telling him he was not the right person to own the firm, the mistake was not firing him on the spot while having coffee and offering him the 50K.

What happened was that for the first four months of 2013, he was taking leads he received from my dinner events that I paid for, and selling the annuities away to another IMO/RIA (insurance marketing organization and Registered Investment Advisor) firm he was planning on moving to. He would send the unsigned applications of new clients to the other company and have the guy there sign them and put everything under his name and then pay my rep leaving me of his pocket for the business. Was this illegal? You bet! Could I have cost him and the other rep stealing the business their licenses and lively-hood? Again, yep! I decided I had no desire to see he or his family sacrificed financially because of a bad move and due to immaturity.

Dummy me! I had so much trust in this young man that I couldn't understand why our sales were so low during that four-month span. He would place all existing client business through our firm in order to show some sales. He just took the new clients and sent them off to his new friend. He also took my entire database off the computer and used it to invite 100% of my clients to his grand opening. I spent 15 hours a day, six days a week, for the next six weeks calling each and every client to save the business.

You might say "Didn't you have a Non-Compete?" Of cours, I did and still do have. I immediately called my attorney who contacted this reps attorney and they battled over the whole thing for three weeks. I found out it is difficult and it takes time to get a cease and desist order out quickly. By the time three weeks had gone by I told my attorney to drop it as the damage had been done by that time.

Ok, you might be saying "Forget this chapter I'm never hiring another rep!" Before you decide that, I want you to know that I now have two new awesome reps in my office who I feel strongly are the right people to be taking over the business. One has been with me for nine years and the other rep, for three years. **This is what allows me to work 25 hours per week and enjoy more of my life.**

THE KEYS TO HIRING AND EMPLOYING OTHER REPS.

1. I would still advise that you have a non-compete signed. While I think they are very hard to enforce, it can be a deterrent.

2. At a point you don't feel a rep you have hired is going to work out or be the kind of person to one day buy and run your firm, let them go quickly. I once heard a person say "Hire slowly and fire quickly".

I think that is good advice. Access each reps DISC score (a personality profile) which you can learn more about at *www.thediscpersonalitytest.com*.

3. The DISC assessment can help you find out what they want **for their future**. Some may not want to own your firm. They love the job and not the pressure of ownership. If you don't intend to sell to them, then this person makes a good fit. The only problem is that the best advisors tend to have the entrepreneurial spirit. So, don't expect a rep with no interest in ownership to do as well as one who is into ownership.

If you do have a rep you intend to sell to someday, don't commit to him on the spot, but do let him know that your intentions are for him to take over someday or at least run a second office for you someday and you will have a loyal person

In closing this chapter, be willing to delegate and let staff people make mistakes if you want to grow. As much as you might not like to, admit it your make mistakes too. Then, don't micro-manage them. Give them a chance to learn and impress you. When they do a good job don't hold back on the praise.

If you hire well, then one day, you can back down the hours you work as you will have developed a fantastic team around you.

CHAPTER NINE:
How to Create Systems and Processes That Run Your Practice and Give You More Free Time. Or, How I Don't Do Paperwork

My team is made up of three advisors (including myself), a Director of Marketing, a COO to run the practice for me and four wonderful and magnificent people in my operations and support area. While your firm may not (and most likely wouldn't be) set up like mine, I hope these job descriptions can help you lay out the processes for your office. I have changed the names of each person for privacy reasons.

MARILYN:

Marilyn is at our front desk (some people like to call her the Director of First Impressions). Here is the list of her roles:

- Answers phones
- Greets clients and prospects and provide them with a menu of goodies available
- Schedule appointments
- Appointment confirmation calls
- Sets up and confirms sales appointment schedules
- Makes and updates labels for mailings
- Maintain sales material inventory (brochures etc.)
- Maintain office equipment
- Front office maintenance
- Filing
- Prepares seminar handouts and necessary equipment
- Allocation letters (for index annuities)
- Address changes
- Creates new files

- Logs new life policies and reviews for accuracy, logs them into CRM and sets up a delivery appointment
- Broadcast to staff company news and events for the week
- Sends out new client surveys
- Sends out 2-week appointment reminders

SUSAN:

Susan is our utility person in the office. Giving her one title hardly covers all that she does. However, the title we gave her is "Portfolio Administrator."

- Operational support: Whatever needs to be done in the operations side of the office that needs help, we call on Susan.
- Opens new accounts online
- Scrubs and processes paperwork for submission
- Maintains and prints out client balance sheets for advisors review meetings with clients.
- Back up to Operations Coordinator

- in handling new application process (advisors don't do paperwork)
- Front desk backup
- Sorts and gets mail to appropriate people
- Beneficiary sheets and changes
- Backup for service to any client needs
- Meets weekly with the operations team
- Assists with phones
- Submits contract delivery sheets to companies

ALICE:

Portfolio Administrator

- Operational support
- Processes and scrubs paperwork when Operations Coordinator is done with it.
- Scrubs, email or Fed-X to investment companies and insurance companies
- Tracks all transfers until in-house
- Research transfer rejects
- Manages business pending report (drawers and files)

- Update new business
- Meets weekly with the operations team
- Cleans up and maintains client investments in CRM
- Email Marilyn to set up clients reviews for first, second year and beyond in CRM
- Maintains and updates sales and production reports

KATHLEEN:

Operations Coordinator

- Takes Gold and Blue sheets from advisors indicating new clients investments to be signed up.
- Prepares all paperwork for client
- Assists in tracking transfers and communicating issues to advisors
- Interfaces with investment and insurance companies to provide additional needs they might have once receiving the applications.
- Handles all deposits and withdrawals by clients

- Handles titling changes in investments and insurance products
- Completes any client requests that come in other than those that are required to be handled by the advisor.
- Maintains client relationships
- Submits contract delivery receipts to companies

While I stated how Susan is a utility personnel, I cannot say enough about the gals that work in our office. They make it a great work environment and the rest of us would be lost without them… each and every one of them.

MORGAN:

Marketing Director

Morgan is the longest running member of our team and the most senior person in the office for about 14 years now. Amongst her role as Marketing Director, she also serves as my personal assistant.

- Travel coordinator
- Oversees my calendar
- Maintains company marketing plan along

with Curt (that's really my name)
- Branding
- Events coordinator
- Directs mail coordinator
- Organizes and books all client events
- Organizes and books all employee and team events
- Sends out flowers, gas cards or baskets to new clients as welcome gifts
- Coordinates referral program
- Arranges monthly marketing seminars and client educational events
- Arranges client seminars
- Works with Curt on marketing materials (and compliance of course)
- Works with outside and inside tech people to keep up website and online resources
- Decorates office for holidays throughout the year
- Maintains Infusionsoft program
- Maintains, manage and runs the company referral program

- Creates newsletters
- Records internal videos and places on our website
- Maintains landing pages
- Purchases food and drink for the front lobby
- Maintains company info email box
- Handles cleaning crew

MIGUEL:

COO/HR/Accounting

- Removes obstacles for Curt
- Execute the business plan (profit/loss)
- Handles internal compliance with rules and regs
- Product due diligence
- Employee/team member communications
- Maintains HR
- Develops and maintains budget
- Be a sounding board for Curt
- Frontline contact with wholesalers and product line reps

- Conducts team meetings
- Firm Liaison with Broker/Dealer
- Payroll
- Operations procedures
- Training and job descriptions
- Accounts receivables
- Accounts payables
- Banking
- Reconciles cash and credit accounts
- Maintains Team member records
- Creates financial reports
- Tracks commissions
- Tracks team vacation days
- Cash flow forecasting
- Handles complex client issues
- All licensing requirements for advisors

BOB AND JOE:

Advisors

- Maintains product knowledge
- Seminar presenters

- Services existing designated clients assigned to them
- Finds and bring on new clients from referrals and seminars
- Creates custom client/prospect presentations using RBG Concepts software
- Develops new leads
- Provides "proactive" customer service
- Develops sales presentations
- Creative marketing ideas
- Serve, serve, serve our clients

CURT WHIPPLE:

Owner

- Establish sales goals
- Product knowledge
- Measures sales results
- Conducts sales meetings with other two reps
- Sales training
- Develops and creates new sales ideas

- Creates sales presentations for one on one meetings using RBG Concepts software
- Creates public seminars
- Creative marketing
- Public speaking
- Client meetings
- Prospect meetings
- Financial Plan creations for each prospect
- Clients review meetings
- Identifies strategic partners and possible joint ventures for the firm
- Investigates new products for possible representation
- Prepares educational workshops for existing clients
- Develops new markets
- Develops corporate strategies
- Serve, serve, serve our clients

BLUE SHEETS AND GOLD SHEETS

Over the years, while working with the team, they designed and came up with the following sheets as forms that our advisors could fill out (the only paperwork I want them to do) and pass the sheets on to the operations team who would produce all of the paperwork for the client to sign.

My goal was that all three advisors spend as much time as possible working with current clients and new prospects and not be buried in paperwork. They are not earning money doing forms because spending much time on doing forms will slow down the progress of the company as a whole.

A copy of each sheet is at the end of the chapter.

Each rep simply fills out a blue sheet for a new client or clients making changes to their portfolio. This informs the operations team what is to be done paperwork wise and the rep goes back to working with clients. The operation team takes care of the rest.

The yellow sheet is for service requests. Some examples might be requesting an RMD withdrawal, needing a check sent, changing beneficiaries or more.

By freeing up the reps, Imagine all three of us making one more sale each month due to the time saved not preparing forms! The average sale in our office is worth between $13,000 and $30,000. Take the low end of that times 3 reps times 12 months and you have an extra $450,000 of revenue per year. How many staff people can you hire for $450,000 per year?

Don't trip over penny's trying to get to dollars!

78 | Abundant Income, Abundant Life!

BLUE SHEET

Chapter Nine | 79

Service Request Form

Income | Withdrawal | Dividend Service Request

General Service Request

Special Instructions

File Name: InvestmentCheckList.xlsx   1/7/2013

GOLD SHEET

CHAPTER TEN:
How Your Office Environment (if you have an office) Can Help You Close Sales

My first office was in the basement of my home. It was cold and dark (a single light bulb) and full of junk (that's my wife's term for everything we tend to collect and no longer have a use for).

Once it became clear I was making a go of it, I somehow talked her into letting me use the corner of the master bedroom (now that's a good wife... or you might now say a dumb wife).

After it became clear that waking up to my office each morning wasn't going to work, I then moved my office into our living room. Although I did have an outside office in 1991 for a brief spell,

I worked out of our living room until we moved to a new home in 1998. The new house allowed me 200 feet of space in my own room for an office and it wasn't until 2002 when I rented an outside office of 750 feet. Things began going so well at this time that 6 months later, I moved to 1,400 feet of office space and finally in December of 2004 I actually built a 3000-foot office space that we still work in to date.

I remember being nervous about the cost of building my own office. In addition to designing the interior, the cost of building out the interior, and purchasing all of the equipment and supplies that would be necessary, I was beginning to freak out wondering if I was in over my head.

One of my staff members at the time came to me and said: "Curt if you would be willing to do this right, this new building will make you a lot of money." I followed through and boy was he ever right.

In the main entrance as you walk in, you will find a waterfall along with decorative plants. When you pass through into the reception area, it is like stepping into the living room of a beautiful home.

KEY: Lots of lamplight.

In the reception are four extremely comfortable chairs and plenty of lamplights. I believe one mistake many advisors make is that their reception area is too professional (or some may say "cold"). They make it modern and have a TV going with market data and nothing but overhead lighting. Our overhead lights are dimmed and we let the lamplight create the atmosphere. The number one thing we hear from our prospects that come in is how comfortable and welcoming our lobby is.

We constantly are baking fresh homemade chocolate chip cookies and filling the air with the smell (talk about tough to resist!). We present each person that comes in with a menu of beverages and snacks that they can enjoy while in the lobby. We have soft music playing in the lobby. We want newcomers to relax! We don't want a pillared and marble office making them nervous about how we will be taking their hard earned money.

I will never forget a time when at 8:10 am our front desk gal "Marilyn" came to me and said "Curt, Mr. _____is in the lobby." I asked her if he had an appointment as our first appointment is usually at 9 am and we don't officially open until 8:30 am. She said she didn't see anything on the calendar for him. I went out to greet him and apologized that I didn't see him on the schedule. His reply was; *"Oh, don't mind me, I just love sitting in your lobby and the chocolate chip cookies and coffee are better than sitting in McDonald's!"* **THAT'S WHAT I'M TALKING ABOUT!**

We went all out on the doors and the wood trim by hiring an Amish carpenter to build each of our office doors in a special wood. We chose calming wallpaper. The desk for each office was classy but not too ornate or large.

Make your office high-end, but comfortable. Don't go too cheap but also, don't go "too professional" and by all means, *lots of lamplight throughout* ***and in every office.***

If you take care and do it right, your office will make you a lot of money. It will say to your prospects that you are here to stay, you are at the top of your industry but most importantly you care about them and want them to feel comfortable and secure with you and your team

CHAPTER ELEVEN:
Why Using the Help of a Coach/Mentor Can Be Key to Your Success.

Why is hiring a Coach/Mentor possibly the smartest decision you could make?

In October 1986, I became a solopreneur (that means no staff… just me). I spent the first five years struggling to pay the bills and support my family… **FIVE YEARS!** Ugh! That was a lot of suffering. Finally, in 1991, I started making a living at least. It wasn't much, but I was finally able to breathe financially. Then from 1991 until 2001 my income "crept" up little by little, but still by 2000 I was frustrated as I had only grown my business to include two part-timers coming into my home office to help me out. 15 years is a long time to keep bumping your head against the wall!

Finally, in 2001, I found the answer to rapid and sustained growth... I found a mentor! Someone who had already laid a path that I could follow without having to hack out my own way. As stated earlier in this book my business income from that point to 2008 grew by tenfold up to $2.7 million of commission and 6 staff. Today, there is 8 others on staff besides me.

> **KEY**: Mentors make it possible for you to do in a few years what can take decades on your own.

Bottom line: Finding (and hiring) a mentor, coach, or consultant is a smart decision. It's an investment you will not regret.

Success leaves clues. You want to take advice from people that are already doing (or have done) what you want to do, not those who aren't where you want to be.

There are no shortcuts.

However, a mentor can help you make better decisions, avoid unnecessary defeats and share ideas and new strategies that can catapult your business in the very first year. A mentor can also help you identify (and make sense of) what you already know, and give you the leverage to take action on the most important pieces. Don't try to reinvent the wheel. Whatever you're trying to do, it's probably already been done before.

A mentor is someone who will give you the unfiltered, unbiased advice that you need most. A mentor is someone who has the experience, expertise, and skills that you wish to acquire.

WHEN TO HIRE A MENTOR

I believe there are two critical and ideal points at which you need to hire a mentor:

1. At the beginning of building a new business.
2. If you've reached a plateau.

Everyone hits a point where they eventually hit a plateau. They've done everything they can with the knowledge and skills they already have. But to become great, you should find out what the champions know that you don't — that's when you get a mentor. I'm sure you've heard before that all of the great athletes in your life have had a mentor. Michael Jordan, Dan Marino, Wayne Gretsky just to name a few.

WHO'S THE RIGHT PERSON FOR YOU?

If you're trying to lose weight or get fit, would you hire an overweight trainer? If you're looking to solve some major life issues, would you hire an inexperienced life coach? If you're trying to become successful in online business, would you hire a mentor that doesn't have an online business?

> **KEY**: Find a mentor who is "Still In The Business".

Too many supposed financial mentors/coaches have decided that *they would rather tell others what to do than do it themselves*. Make sure you find a mentor who not only has done it **but is still doing it** and can not only tell you what to do but demonstrate to you what to do. Make sure you ask questions about their past success. **If they were so successful, what made them stop and become a mentor?**

Note: Don't be the person who asks for time and expertise for nothing. Make sure you plan on paying for mentoring and coaching. If you have the right person in mind, but you find out they don't have a formal mentoring program, make sure you offer to pay them.

Find someone you can build a personal relationship with. Be careful about signing up with generic companies that offer "coaching for everyone". I've seen it where the mentor in the videos online sells you on their plan and then you get one of the cohorts who frankly may not have EVER even been in your business or business for themselves. Why not decide on your own and pick exactly who you want to work with? I think that's more of a win-win situation for everyone.

PAYING YOUR MENTOR?

A professional mentor, coach, or consultant will already have fixed costs for their services. You'll find that some will charge as little as $500 a month, while others will charge even $10,000 to $25,000 or more. I personally know one mentor/coach of financial advisors who charges $12,000 per month with a one year contract to coach. He's not even a financial advisor and certainly is not still in the business as an active rep. **BEWARE**: *A consultant's cost is not always directly proportional to their ability to generate results.*

CONCLUSION

Investing in information that helps you grow and get results is the best type of investment you can make. If the time is right, you have clear expectations/goals, and you've identified a solid candidate — you should look into hiring them.

TEN REASONS WHY HIRING A MENTOR IS A MUST!

As an entrepreneur, it's exciting to go into it alone and create something on your own. However, the reality is that, while you have a great idea, you may not know exactly what you should be doing with your business and at which time to develop it into a sustainable business.

Here are ten other reasons why you need someone like a mentor/coach:

1. Mentors provide information and knowledge. As Benjamin Franklin said,

    "Tell me and I forget, teach me and I may remember, involve me and I learn."

    When I was starting out, I had no idea what was involved in running a business, including making a business plan, budgeting, handling daily operations, making strategic decisions or running a marketing campaign. With a mentor, you can tap into a wealth of knowledge to get up to speed faster and shorten that learning curve.

2. Mentors can see where we need to improve where we often cannot. Moviemaker George Lucas noted, "Mentors have a way of seeing more of our faults than we would have like to. It's the only way we grow." They will always be brutally honest with you and tell you exactly how it is rather than downplay any weaknesses they see in you.

3. Mentors find ways to stimulate our personal and professional growth. Another famous movie director explained, *"The delicate balance of mentoring someone is not creating them in my image, but giving them the opportunity to create themselves."*

4. Mentors offer encouragement and help us to keep going. Oprah Winfrey once stated, "A mentor is someone who allows

you to see the hope inside yourself." They are there, no matter what, and offer moral support sprinkled heavily with cheerleading. There were times that, if there wasn't a mentor there for me, I could have easily, "caved-in," emotionally, or given up on the business. However, I had a mentor and each one I had wouldn't let me stop but provided the encouragement and guidance that gave me hope and confidence that I could do whatever was asked of me.

5. Mentors are disciplinarians that create necessary boundaries that we cannot set for ourselves. Being an entrepreneur can be challenging when it comes to self-motivation and self-discipline. A mentor will teach you good work habits and provide the boundaries for you to work within. This will solidify your work ethic, sharpen your focus and clarify your priorities in a way that is tough to do on your own.

6. Mentors are sounding boards so we can bounce ideas off them for an unfiltered

opinion. **I have always been guilty at chasing shiny objects.** If I read or saw something that I thought was awesome and would mean either more growth or better value for my clients, I would run after it, buy it and start off to implement it. Then before I would see it through, I would run off chasing the next shiny object. My staff had a pony toy and whenever I would bring a new bright idea to them, they would come marching into my office, pulling on the reins of the horse saying "Whoa Boy! Whoa Boy!" My staff would help me talk through the opportunities and they helped me see which ones had potential and why others were better left alone. I appreciated their candor because I might have otherwise pursued a business idea that had no legs.

7. Mentors are trusted advisers. In the world of business, it can be hard to know who to trust - and that you can trust someone, especially with proprietary information or intellectual property. Since a mentor can be an objective third-party with no stake

in any idea or venture, they are free to let you know what they think. In return, you can trust that they will keep everything you share confidential.

8. Mentors can be connectors. Playing a dual role of teacher and connector, a mentor can provide access to those within your industry that are willing to invest in your company, offer their skills and expertise, introduce you to talents that can fuel your business and help you get closer to your target audience.

9. Mentors have the experiences you can learn from to prevent making the same mistakes beginners make. Starting a business is challenging enough, so if you can skip doing things the hard way, why wouldn't you? A mentor has been there, right where you are, and has made numerous mistakes that they can now use as a basis for helping you skip the devastating effects of learning the hard way.

10. Mentors are priceless in more ways than one. Typically, a mentoring relationship

will grow organically through connections within your industry and network. A mentor should not do it solely for the money. Instead, they are driven by the satisfaction of helping another entrepreneur, paying it forward from a similar experience they had when starting their own business.

Having a mentor is not a sign of weakness; it shows you are smart enough, passionate and are driven enough to succeed.

CHAPTER TWELVE:
Finding the Right
Insurance Marketing Organization

I have been with several Insurance Marketing Organizations (IMO) which are sometimes referred to as Field Marketing Organizations (FMO) throughout my career. My understanding is that if they only offer insurance services, they are an IMO and if they offer securities branch as well, then they are an FMO. Regardless, for this discussion, I will use the term IMO.

The first IMO I went with taught me how to do seminars. The second one taught me about taxes. The third and fourth one were extremely large and seemed to offer me all anyone would want from an IMO. However, I found the last two lacking in personal service. I felt like another number and not very important. Now, I have what I feel is the best IMO for me!

I wanted this chapter to be about what to look for in an IMO and how to make sure it is the right fit for you.

1. The first key is to understand what it is that you need help with and how much personal attention you desire in order to implement what it is you endeavor to achieve as an agent or advisor.
2. Align your need with the value proposition of the IMO. Yes, ask for one and see what it says. If they don't have one, that's a red flag!
3. How are they going to service you? At the beginning, with one of the largest IMO's I have been with, I was given an internal contact person that would be the person who would focus on helping me. However, as they grew larger, I then found myself dealing with the assistant to my contact.

4. Look into what carriers the IMO represents and be certain they have all of the products you need. I like using annexus products for annuities. Not all IMO's are contracted with them and therefore I would keep looking.

5. Make sure to ask if the IMO is independent or owned by a carrier. If they are owned by a certain carrier, I would move on as they most likely will always sway you to their carrier's products. They may also struggle to do what they would normally want to do and recommend to you as the carrier now controls decisions

6. An important one to check right up front is how the IMO handles a potential release request. Some IMO's may hold you hostage and not release your contract with an insurance company, thus, forcing you to write for companies you would not usually write business for. You want it in writing that they will not hold you hostage should your relationship with them not work out

7. All IMO's will offer you marketing support. Don't just talk about marketing support on the phone with them. Make sure you get it in writing what "Marketing Support" really means. If they reimburse you or bonus you based on the business you write, is that for all carriers? Is it different depending on the carrier you choose to do business with? Getting this straight up front saves a lot of heart-ache and frustration once you contract with them.

8. Find out if they have any costs or production requirements or guidelines for any commitments they make to you. There are too many instances where something stated on the phone changes once you sign the agreement. **GET IT IN WRITING! I MEAN EVERYTHING THEY COMMIT TO YOU IN WRITING!**

9. Ask for references of other agents that they work with who are producing roughly the same amount of production that you are producing. Of course, they will give you referrals to the agents who

love them the most. These may be their largest agents or reps that don't need a lot of help. However, sometimes it is surprising what another agent may tell you that the IMO wouldn't have contemplated. If you are currently producing a lower amount of business (you wouldn't be in their top 20% of producers) make sure to ask each reference they give you what their annual production is. If it is quite a bit more than your current production, they may not be the best reference. However, if they are producing more than you currently are, ask what their production was BEFORE coming to the IMO you are considering. If they did two million before and now do 10 million that could be a good sign.

10. Ensure you ask if there is any cost to you for any marketing system they provide. Also, ask if there is a production requirement in order to get and keep those systems.

11. Bigger does not always mean the best! Don't get hung up on the size of the IMO.

12. Take advantage of a free trip to the perspective IMO. A visit to their home office will allow you to meet the people that you may end up working with and gain a better understanding of how the IMO works. To me, it is important to ask questions about the people in top management and their families. It is important to get them out of the "business" mindset and into more personal things. It is important to know the owner's character. You can get to know this better by meeting them outside their office for a meal and asking questions. This can tell me a lot about how they run their business.

13. Nowadays it is important to know the IMO's compliance protocols. What do they expect from you and what can you expect from them to make sure you are protected and safe from any regulatory issues.

14. What ongoing education does the IMO provide? Will this cost you something? If you have to fly to these educational

events, is this on their dime? What is the content of the meetings? Make sure when you talk to references that you ask them about the meetings and do they find them worthwhile.

15. Coaching and mentoring can be a huge bonus. Many IMO's say they have great mentoring and coaching programs. The best are the ones that offer full time in-house coaching as well as mentoring and coaching by currently active and successful reps in the field.

16. Ask them for a detailed plan on how they intend to help you grow your business.

17. **GET IT IN WRITING, GET IT IN WRITING, GET IT IN WRITING!**

CHAPTER THIRTEEN:
Looking Forward to Monday

I have a friend named Adam Witty who is CEO of Advantage Media. Advantage is a company that helps build "Authority Marketing" for anyone interested in doing so. I believe Adam was born with entrepreneurial blood running through his veins. In the last ten years, Adam has taken his company from nothing to $35 million per year in sales. Without a doubt in my mind, by 2021, I believe his company will exceed $100 million per year. The reason I bring Adam up is that I would like to borrow the title of his most recent book "Looking Forward to Monday" (which I highly recommend you read) for the title of this last chapter.

How do you look at Mondays?

I remember in my not too distant past of how Mondays even had a way of ruining my Sundays. I was always giddy on Fridays because I made it through another week! Then long about Sunday around 5-6pm, I would get a pit in my stomach as I thought about going back into the office on Monday and starting all over again.

The pressure was immense! I knew I had to provide for my family. The problem I had at that time was the assurance of how to do so when I didn't have enough people to talk to.

I didn't have a prospecting "System" that worked. I didn't have a referral "System" that worked. I didn't have a staff to help me as I didn't feel I could afford anyone on staff. I didn't have a mentor or a coach. **I FELT ALONE AND SCARED!**

Another reason some reps don't look forward to Mondays is that they aren't working in the area of their natural gifts. I am a creative person who loves to serve others. I love to solve problems that others may face (that's where I had to learn to at times just listen to my wife and not try to solve her problems). I love building a business and constantly looking for ways to make it better and more effective for our clients. **WHAT I DON'T LIKE, ENJOY OR FEEL I AM NECESSARILY GOOD AT IT, IS MANAGING PEOPLE!** I found myself at one point hating Mondays because I had to manage people.

As you strive to build your business, make sure you stay in the areas of your unique ability. Anything that needs to be done outside of your most gifted area can always be done better by someone else. You may not believe that another person can do something as good as you can and they may not do it the same way you would. However, you will be happier by letting things outside your unique ability go to another person and so will your clients.

Finally, let me again emphasize the value of being in a good mastermind group or what I call a MasterClass (which involves more training in addition to sharing ideas with one another) with your peers. *It is by far the most inexpensive way for you to get the education you need to grow.*

When it comes to marketing, you can learn what works and doesn't work through the school of hard knocks and waste tens of thousands of dollars. Or you can find out from your masterclass group and mentor what works best for them and simply duplicate it.

When it comes time to hire staff it can be an answer to prayers or it can be the first step to the pit of hell. The wrong person can ruin your office atmosphere and undermine your authority. Talk about **STRESS!** A masterclass group can help you make better decisions on when you should hire and who you should hire.

When it comes to making important decisions, having a masterclass team to run your options through and help guide you through your decisions can be priceless.

When you are having trouble generating enough leads, a masterclass team can share how they successfully get their leads.

When you are having trouble closing a particular sale, the masterclass team and your coach will be there to help you over the hump.

When you just need friends to share frustrations with, your masterclass team can be there.

I promise you that the cost of being in a masterclass group compared to all of the dollars you will waste or lose by not having a masterclass group will save you hundreds of thousands of dollars. You will build your business more quickly, more efficiently and more profitably so that you can enjoy life, enjoy your family and enjoy Monday mornings again.

If you would like more information on joining a "MasterClass" group of agents and advisors, please visit: www.myadvisorsuccess.com

New masterclass groups are forming each month. Don't delay, do it today!

May God "Richly" bless your future!

"As iron sharpens iron, so one man sharpens another."

— Proverbs 27:17 (NIV)

Yours for greater success!

Curt Whipple

Curt Whipple, CWS, CEP

CHAPTER FOURTEEN:
Final Thoughts: How I Found Success In Life

I felt compelled to leave you not so much with another chapter as some final thoughts about life. *In this section, I will share with you the greatest secret of my success.* However, I must begin this chapter with a warning label. I have no intention of holding anything back. It is my story. Therefore, it may not be what you would expect. But to write it with anything less than the truth or what it is or was would be an injustice.

Depending on your background, your faith, and your upbringing, you may find some of this offensive or uncomfortable. I apologize in advance if this is the case. However, it's my story. If you would be easily offended, then please stop now and read no further. If you stop reading at this time, thank you for allowing me the privilege of sharing and having a part in your life. I trust the information provided has helped and will continue to help you find financial freedom.

Now, for those of you still with me, allow me to share something greater than financial freedom. In order to convey the secret to my success, I need to go back in time a bit.

When I was younger, I was blessed with parents who constantly encouraged me and told me how I could do most anything and how great of a success I would be someday. I eventually began to believe it and anytime something good happened in my life, I would say "Gee, look at that, my folks must be right!" Maybe I am going to be successful!" It wasn't that I didn't make a ton of mistakes and do things wrong, I just focused on and hung on to those things I did right.

The successes built on themselves, especially in the early years. Out of four children born to Marvin and Norah Whipple, I was the only one who finished college. It's not because I was better or smarter than my brothers and sisters, it was because I "had" to finish college. Let me explain. I had a dream in my heart that was planted when I was sixteen years old. I decided that I wanted to be a disc jockey on the radio. However, then it went further. I also decided to own and run 14 radio stations across the United States. Why 14? At the time, it was the maximum amount you could own by law. I had intended these radio stations to be such that they would have a "positive" impact on the lives of young people across America. An impact that would help kids and young adults learn and believe that they could find success and happiness in life. Hang in there, later, I'll tell you how financial planning came into the picture.

While in college, I worked at the college's radio station, and then, miracles began to happen. I did some on airtime and creative work with my professor, Dr. Tom Nash at Biola University. He quickly became one of my heroes in life. Dr. Nash asked me if I would help, by trying to sell some advertising time around the community to help raise money and support the station. Now, the station only reached the students on campus. So, I decided at first to stick with the local retailers interested in reaching the student body.

One day, I decided to call an advertising agency in Los Angeles. Here's this tiny little school of 4,500 students and I'm calling an ad agency with the marble counters on the top floor of a Los Angeles skyscraper. To my amazement, I got the appointment and even more surprisingly, I got the account. My sales success was so great, that I continued to build the revenues for our little station, beyond everyone's expectations. In my senior year, I decided to approach a "real" radio station off campus about selling for them part-time. I got the job at KYMS in Santa Ana and sold so many ads, that I was equaling the sales of the full-timers on a part-time basis. After graduation, I married my sweetheart, Connie Johnson, back in Michigan and we moved to California where I worked full time in radio sales. Immediately, I began meeting with a college buddy named Wally Hollis. He and I began putting together a proposal to buy and own our first station at the ripe ages of 23 and 22. We identified a station in Detroit, Michigan (I thought we'd start with a tiny market) that I had spoken to the owner and was given the impression we could buy for $3.5 million. In 1980, that was a bunch of money! We spent over 6 months preparing the presentation and plan.

There was only one problem. Where would two college grads, come up with $3.5 million? According to a bank that showed any interest at all, we would have to come up with one million dollars of down payment, in order to have a chance of financing the rest. While in college, I met a guy who had an uncle in Michigan who ran a rather large drapery business. I called his Uncle and asked if we could meet, explaining the idea and a potential ownership position in the new station. He said he would listen so Wally, my wife Connie and I flew to Detroit to stay with her parents and make our "pitch".

As we walked into the meeting, the drapery owner and his right-hand man walked into the room and were immediately set back by our apparent youth. I guess they were expecting more. However, by the end of the meeting, they committed $100,000 to the two young college grads! Not knowing where else to go, we asked them if they knew any other business owners that may be willing to listen to the same opportunity. They gave us the names of two brothers and a sister who owned auto parts stores in the metro area. Again, they were met with surprise, due to our age. However, by the time we were done, they committed $300,000 to the plan. By the end of the two weeks, we had raised $500,000 of the $1,000,000 needed. However, we ran out of time and needed to get back to our jobs in L.A. We decided to come back and find the other $500,000 in two weeks.

During the two weeks in L.A., I received notice that the station we had planned to purchase was sold to Doubleday Broadcasting for $8.3 million! We lost our bid.

I remained at KYMS for a while and almost immediately became a sales manager. Times were good, Connie was working at Ford Aerospace in Newport Beach and we both enjoyed a beautiful new home, more income than we could have dreamed of, a 280-Z as a company car at the radio station and did I say more money than we could have dreamed of? We were making about $75,000 per year combined. In 1979, that was a lot of money! However, the dream of developing stations to having a positive impact on young people was still lingering in my heart.

I felt it was important, that if I was going to run stations of my own, I better get some experience as a station manager, rather than only a sales manager. I was reading Broadcasting Magazine and I noticed an ad for a General Manager (GM) position at a station in the St. Louis, MO market. I was 26 years old. I didn't know it, but that was considered way too young to have any hope of getting a position in radio broadcasting like that, especially in a top 20 market at the time. People my age would consider themselves lucky to get a General Manager job in ANY town, even Podunk, USA.

Still, I applied for the job. By this time, I was getting used to the shocks and looks I would receive when people and station staff first met me and realized my age. Yep! I got the same look on this interview. Skipping the details, I got the job! To my knowledge, I was the youngest GM in a top 20 market anywhere in the country.

Sounds like life was just too good to be true. Things were going great. I was moving up the ladder, and in my eyes, there was no stopping me.

THE BAD TIMES BEGIN!

The station I took the GM job was not one of the strongest stations in ST. Louis... OK, it was pathetic! It was ranked 42 out of 42 in the ST. Louis ARB ratings. Didn't scare me any! I had just come from one of the top stations in Orange County, California. I was so confident in my abilities by this point, that I know this is where God decided it was time to allow me to learn that ultimately, it wasn't all up to me and I couldn't do it all by myself. Also, it's where my lessons in financial freedom and managing others began to build.

As Connie and I began to look for our new home in ST. Louis, we settled on one across the Mississippi River in Belleville, Illinois. It was a gorgeous house that frankly, we didn't need but fell in love with. It was more than we could afford at the time. However, I had been promised bonuses on any business generated above the current cash flow of the station and just knew I would have the station "rockin' and rollin'" in no time at all. So, I bought the house. Though the station immediately started growing in listeners, it wasn't growing as quickly as I had hoped. Income was still not up to par and Connie had just given birth to our daughter, Kelly. As parents, we felt strongly about the importance of Connie being a full-time Mom and therefore, went from the two big incomes in California to just the one small one in ST, Louis, with a HUGE mortgage on our new home. The home that I felt would be the envy of our friends became our most humiliating and humbling embarrassment. We purchased the home in 1981 and if you're old enough, you'll remember the double-digit inflation and interest rates back at that time. Our home mortgage was at a very high interest rate and resulted in outrageous payments each month. As a result, we lived in a "palace" with virtually no furniture. We couldn't afford to buy any furniture. We lived in a fishbowl, as we couldn't afford drapes. One day, while eating dinner, we both jumped, as a total stranger walked up on the deck (came with the house) out the back sliding doors and pushed his face up against the glass. With cupped hands around his eyes, he was staring into our kitchen, trying to get a glimpse of the inside of this empty house that surely must be for sale. Both parties were embarrassed.

I came back home from work one day and found Connie sitting on the love seat (the only piece of furniture we had outside of the kitchen and bedroom), crying because that day, she had received 5 phone calls from creditors demanding payments on the credit cards.

I KNEW SOMETHING HAD TO BE DONE!

Pressures were beginning to grow. The station was not performing as well as I had planned and the owners were beginning to put the squeeze on me to put more and more "garbage" on the air, just to make more money. It was about that time, that I had an old friend come by and offer to sell me some life insurance. Not knowing I didn't have a dime to put toward it, he made his best pitch. This was "cool" life insurance, called Universal Life. It was brand new at the time, and you actually could make money and build your financial future by owning it. I asked my friend how much he made by selling it and then asked if they were hiring part-time salespeople. I got the job on a part-time basis while still working in radio and immediately found some small success. We began paying off some bills and eventually, I was made an offer to come full time in life insurance sales. I had to do something to stop the financial pain and free my wife from the creditors. I was getting the squeeze from the owners at the station and decided it was time to move on and go where I felt I could support the family.

I'll never forget the day I came home from the radio station with the decision to enter the life insurance business full time. I don't ever recall crying so hard and shedding so many tears. The dream, for now, had died!

Too much more of my story, I'm afraid, would cause great pain for you to read… in more ways than one. I quickly went from life insurance sales to financial planning and in 1986, began my own financial planning firm, C. Curtis & Associates. Each step along the way has been filled with failures yet many successes as well.

The point to all of this is that I found, in my own strength I am very limited. No matter how good I think I am… or how bad, there had to be more to life than just money and climbing the corporate ladder. I always felt that the more money I made the greater of a success I would become. The bigger my house, the fancier the car, the grander the trips and vacations, the more of a success I would be. But what happens when I die? Do I take it with me? Is life about how much money I can accumulate? Or, is there more?

By no means have I ever been financially rich as most would see it? Compared to modern day athletes and movie stars and large corporate executives, I was a little guy. Oh, but how I wanted to swim with the big fish. I wanted to swim with them so bad, I was willing to ruin my life, and the lives of the ones I loved the most, trying to get it.

As a financial planner, I have sat with people who were multi-millionaires to those totally broke and realized they could be equally unhappy, regardless of their level of income or position. As a matter of fact, in many cases, I found the wealthy ones tended to be unhappier than the ones without any money. I've known friends who were well off financially and yet still miserable. If money buys happiness, why are so many wealthy people ruining their lives with it? You see, the truly rich people will tell you money is only important to a certain point. Once you have enough of it, it just doesn't matter anymore. It's not important. That's why rich people can be miserable. Because, their whole life, they've lived by the misconception that money buys happiness. When they finally get the money and they still aren't happy, then they begin trying all sorts of weird stuff to find happiness. It's why so many famous and rich people ultimately sink their own ship. So if money and fame aren't the answer to happiness, what is?

First, don't get me wrong; we should always strive to be financially free. Financial freedom can mean no bondage to creditors. The point is we don't have to be financially rich to be financially free. However, there's one more thing to add.

Along my journey, I was also developing a closer "relationship" with God. Note, I didn't say religion, rather a relationship. This relationship in itself is a lifelong journey, it never ends. With each year of my life that passes by, the relationship tends to grow stronger and deeper. Each time I begin to think I'm wise, I quickly realize there is much more to learn. I'm sure this will continue until the day I die.

Have you ever noticed that at each stage of life, you sometimes think how ignorant you were when you were younger? At 21, I thought I was so mature. I would look back at the high schoolers (who thought they knew it all) and think of how immature they were. At 35, I couldn't believe how naive I was at 21. I think you get my point. The same seems to be true of my relationship with God. At each stage of my life, I would have times that I thought I had it all together. I felt in communion with God, family relationships were strong, and financially, things were good. It would always seem about then, that I would learn another lesson in life.

Connie and I have two of the most beautiful children you can imagine. Inside and out, our children constantly bring us happiness as parents. They've made their mistakes and caused us grief at times, as any teenager or child would. But overall, we couldn't imagine two children providing us with greater joy. Are our children this way because we were such awesome parents? No way! We did our best. However, the results are truly a blessing of God and He gets all the credit.

Whenever our toughest times and lessons in life surfaced, we would find ourselves looking for answers in the Bible. The closer our relationship with God would be, the more peace, joy, and happiness we would find. Then, things may get going really good again, and suddenly, God was in the back seat. It was as if I was saying, "OK God, thanks for getting me this far, I can take it from here!" Then, after time doing it my way, I would once again mess it all up and it was time to seek God again.

I have found God to be real and living and very much involved in my life. He is anxious to be part of your life regardless of your past. It's through this relationship, that Connie and I have found true happiness. However, it comes from a source we seldom think of... our creator.

Financial freedom can add to our family's happiness, being financially rich doesn't. In Philippians 4:12 & 13 of the Bible, Paul says, *"I know what it is to be in need and I know what it is to have plenty. I have learned the secret of being **content in any and every situation**, whether well fed or hungry, whether living in plenty or in want. I can do all things through Him who gives me strength."* It is in this relationship with God that happiness is found. You can't take all your wealth with you when you die. I heard it said once that I've never seen a Brinks truck following a Hurst. I've also heard it said that money just shifts from one person to the next. As we journey through life, we accumulate money. Then when we die, the money is dispersed to others and the cycle starts all over again. However, no one ever really "owns" it.

Are you trying to find happiness by obtaining more money? Read the magazines! Read about the lives of so many who do have the money. Are they truly the happiest people? Or, are those who have a relationship with family, those financially free and those who have a relationship with their creator the ones who are truly rich and successful in life?

In Mark 8:36 it says:

> "What good is it for a man to gain the whole world, yet forfeit his own soul?"

Are you spending all of your time trying to get more money? Take a look around you. You'll find more treasure than you could ever imagine, right within your own household, your own family, and a relationship with God.

I have found my relationship with God comforts me in times of stress, worry, anxiety, and fear. If you would like to know more about this relationship, I would like to recommend a book.

The Great Exchange by Jerry Bridges

I know the ideas presented in the book you just read can lead you to unlimited income and more free time. Now it's up to you. Will you use them?

While finding your way and success you desire may take time, it will happen if you're patient. The Living Bible says:

> *"But these things I plan won't happen right away. Slowly, steadily, surely, the time approaches when the vision will be fulfilled. If it seems slow, do not despair, for these things will surely come to pass. Just be patient! They will not be overdue by a single day."*
>
> — Habakkuk 2:3

Now, allow me to leave you with this prayer found in Colossians 1:11&12.

> *We pray that you will be filled with his mighty, glorious strength so that you can keep going, no matter what happens – always full of the joy of the Lord, and always thankful to the Father, who has made us fit to share all the wonderful things that belong to those who live in the kingdom of light.*

May God richly bless you and yours. May you find financial freedom and the true riches you seek in life.

www.ingramcontent.com/pod-product-compliance
Lightning Source LLC
Chambersburg PA
CBHW060847220526
45466CB00003B/1272